ULTIMATE TASTY HIGH-PROTEIN HEALTHY, LOW-CARB METABOLISM SMOOTHIES

Heather DiBiasi, MS, RDN

FAIR WINDS

Quarto.com

First Published in 2024 by Fair Winds Press,
an imprint of The Quarto Group,
100 Cummings Center, Suite 265-D,
Beverly, MA 01915, USA.
T (978) 282-9590 F (978) 283-2742

Fair Winds Press titles are also available at discount for retail, wholesale, promotional, and bulk purchase. For details, contact the Special Sales Manager by email at specialsales@quarto.com or by mail at The Quarto Group, Attn: Special Sales Manager, 100 Cummings Center, Suite 265-D, Beverly, MA 01915, USA.

28 27 26 25 24 1 2 3 4 5

ISBN: 978-0-7603-9334-5

Digital edition published in 2024
eISBN: 978-0-7603-8500-5

The content in this book was previously published as *Protein Power Smoothies* by Heather DiBiasi (Fair Winds Press 2024).

Library of Congress Cataloging-in-Publication Data available under *Protein Power Smoothies* (Fair Winds Press 2024).

Design and page layout: Laura Shaw Design
Photography: Maria Siriano
Illustration: Shutterstock

Printed in China

CONTENTS

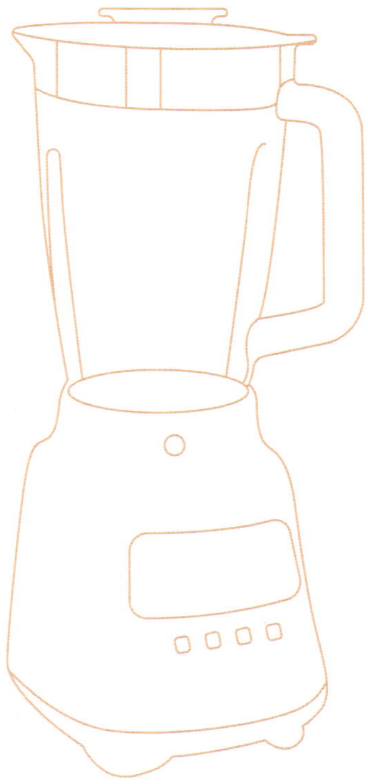

INTRODUCTION

AFTER YOU DRINK A SMOOTHIE, do you count down the minutes until lunch or sneak frequent peeks into the pantry? If so, then you've probably had what I like to call a sugar bomb!

Most smoothies you see online or in local smoothie shops start with a banana here, add in a few dates there, and blend it up with the latest "health" trend such as oat milk (aka more carbs and some inflammatory oils). From a macronutrient perspective, they might as well be serving you an ice cream sundae. In reality, ice cream might even contain more protein than most of your typical smoothies! Feeling intense food cravings just one hour after drinking a smoothie is a signal that your smoothie was not made correctly for you. Even though you had the best intentions for doing something good for your body, combining a bunch of otherwise healthy ingredients like pineapple, mango, and a banana and pulsing them up with fruit juice actually negatively impacts both your metabolic health and weight loss.

These high-carb, low-protein smoothies are digested rapidly in our body and spike our blood sugar. And what goes up must come down, right? Typically, this spike is followed by a crash. We feel tired, we're irritable, and we're on a ravenous search for more sugar to pick us back up. Cue thoughts of "Omigosh, it's only 11 a.m.? Why am I already so hungry? What's for lunch?" and "Damn, why did Sally have to bring those doughnuts to the office? I cannot stop thinking about them. Maybe I should just grab one!" We find our mind starting to drift as we think about our next meal or snack every few minutes instead of focusing on the work we're trying to get done or the conversations we are trying to have. We become hormonally hungry, which makes it feel almost impossible to say "no, thank you" to those more indulgent or carbohydrate-heavy foods, foods we don't really want to eat but now all of a sudden we can't stop thinking about. But I'm here to tell you that it's not you; it's your blood sugar talking.

Blood sugar spikes in response to a high-carb, low-protein meal can also trigger inflammation and shift the body into storage mode, turning off our ability to burn fat for a period of time. Just because these foods are healthy doesn't mean it's healthy to heap them together in a pile and blend them up. Have you ever heard that too much of a good thing isn't always so good? This is a perfect example of that.

However, this unhealthy cycle can be changed. Smoothies can be your secret weapon for staying full so you are not counting down the minutes until lunch, a snack, or dinner. Properly constructed smoothies help you take control of your health and optimize your metabolism even while you shed pounds, if you want to.

My low-carb, high-protein smoothie formula fuels the body so it can function at its best while keeping you full and efficiently burning fat. These smoothies have not only assisted me with my own weight-loss journey, but they have helped hundreds of my clients lose weight and improve their lab values while staying full and energized throughout the day. When you set the tone for the day with a high-protein, low-carbohydrate smoothie, it can help to regulate your hunger, making you feel like you are in control of your body and food choices instead of feeling like your body is bossing you around.

How to Use This Smoothie Book

This book can be the starting point to your new healthy lifestyle or a nice upgrade to the healthy lifestyle you may currently have. If you really want to get the most out of this book, I highly suggest implementing some of the recipes for breakfast each day as soon as possible, starting with flavors that truly speak to your taste buds.

As you begin to implement these recipes and feel the amazing benefits, read all the chapters. I repeat, do not skip any chapters! I promise you, there is a method in my madness. I know it can be tempting to skip the reading all together and get straight to the recipes, but the chapters are truly where the magic lies. And if you don't believe in magic, then you'll at least appreciate the science.

Although the smoothie recipes in this book are designed to flip that physiological and behavioral switch to your meal choices and habits, the reading portion is designed to flip the psychological switch, which is how long-term change actually occurs. Just drinking the smoothies is great, but understanding why you are drinking them is what gives you the power to control your health. When you understand the science behind your high-protein, low-carbohydrate smoothies and you know how to use the formula to make unlimited options, I am confident that you will feel empowered to continue drinking these smoothies. And the truth is, these smoothies are just the start. As you start to really appreciate first-hand that you are doing something good for your health and feeling amazing along the way, it will help facilitate other healthy behaviors to follow. This is truly not your ordinary smoothie book. So, grab your blender, put your reading glasses on, and get ready to have your mind and taste buds blown!

1

SMOOTHIE SCIENCE

YOU'RE PROBABLY WONDERING by now *why* your smoothies should be high protein and low carb. Maybe you've heard some information (true or not) about high-protein and low-carb lifestyles and also about how smoothies are a healthy option for a meal or snack. Yet most smoothies at cafés or online are sugar bombs that barely have any protein. They are just setting the stage for failure.

I want to help you understand not only how to make a balanced smoothie (which we will definitely be covering more in depth in the next chapter) but also why it is important that your smoothie is balanced. If there is one thing I've learned from working with hundreds of clients—as well as my own personal and professional experience—knowing the why behind our choices helps motivate us to make the changes we want. It's much more effective than just doing what someone says because they said so. In this chapter, we are going to break down the science behind your food choices so you feel motivated from the inside out to make these changes in your life!

Blood Sugar Balance

You need to understand blood sugar balance to understand how to build a healthy, high-protein, low-carb smoothie. When our smoothies are in balance, our blood sugar is in balance, and so our body is in balance.

Our bodies are actually always working hard to stay in equilibrium. One of their top priorities is keeping our blood sugar within a normal range. This is not only true for people with diabetes; this is true for every single living, breathing person. Basically, if you have a pulse, this should matter to you. To survive, our body needs to regulate our blood sugar. And what we eat (or drink) on a daily basis can either help to support this balance or force our body to work hard to regulate it. To optimize our health, it's important to eat in a way that supports our metabolic processes, including blood sugar regulation. And who wouldn't want to support our own body? After all, it is our home.

The Three Musketeers: Protein, Fat, and Carbohydrates

We get our energy from three macronutrients: protein, fat, and carbohydrates. To optimize our blood sugar, we have to understand how these energy sources metabolize in the body and how they affect our blood sugar.

What About Fiber?

Fiber is the nondigestible part of a carbohydrate that for the most part does not break down to blood sugar. I'll go into this more soon, but choosing higher-fiber sources of carbohydrates will help mediate carbs' effect on blood sugar. Because vegetables are mainly composed of fiber, they have little to no impact on blood sugar. However, starches or fruits have significantly less fiber compared with the total number of carbs, so they will raise blood sugar despite their fiber content. Although there is no need to completely eliminate these foods from your diet—and I don't recommend that—it is important to understand that starch and fruit still raise blood sugar and should be portioned for blood sugar balance.

Once we consume food, it is digested and broken down into smaller particles:

→ Proteins break down into amino acids.

→ Fats break down into fatty acids.

→ And carbohydrates break down into glucose (aka blood sugar).

Because carbohydrates break down to blood sugar, they are the macronutrient that most impacts our blood sugar response. Protein, fat, and fiber do not directly break down to blood sugar, so they have little to no effect on our blood sugar.

Do you remember the show *The Magic School Bus,* where the students go on bus rides to learn about different science topics? Let's take our own trip on that magic school bus and visualize what happens in the body when we drink smoothies that are low in protein and high in carbohydrate versus smoothies that are high in protein and low in carbohydrate.

The Problem with High-Carbohydrate, Low-Protein Smoothies

Think about a smoothie that is mainly made up of fruit juice and fruits such as banana, berries, dates, and pineapple. Although it might be tasty, this smoothie is primarily carbohydrates with little to no protein or fat. This is a typical smoothie you might see in a café, and it could contain anywhere from 50 to a whopping 100 grams (or sometimes more) of sugar! There will be some fiber in this smoothie, but not enough to counteract the high amounts of carbohydrates that go along with it. A high-carb, low-protein smoothie like this will digest rapidly in our body, breaking down to mainly blood sugar because it is mostly carbohydrates. This leads to a swift and hefty spike in our blood sugar, and because smoothies are liquid and predigested, they have an even steeper impact on our blood sugar response than if we had eaten the fruits whole and had to break them down ourselves.

When our blood sugar spikes, our body gets a little dramatic. Sirens go off, telling our body to lower its blood sugar. This signal triggers the pancreas to overproduce a hormone called insulin, which helps pick up the blood sugar from our bloodstream and place it into our cells. You can think of insulin like the mail carrier trying to help deliver packages to your door or, in this case, sugar to our cells.

This spike is followed by a crash about 90 minutes later, once our body has used or stored the blood sugar, leaving us feeling tired, irritable, and on a ravenous search for more carbs to pick our blood sugar back up. That process is referred to as reactive hypoglycemia. Reactive hypoglycemia is why, not long after a high-carb smoothie or meal, you might feel extremely hungry or you might get intense cravings for more sugar or carbs while simultaneously wanting to take a nap. It's actually very similar to a hangover—the party was fun at the time, yet you're reaching for that mimosa the next day at brunch to make you feel good again in the midst of your headache and nausea. However, instead of looking for another drink to kill the hangover, you're looking for more carbs. This all happens within a span of just a few hours. What a buzzkill, huh?

Reactive hypoglycemia also makes it easy to feel out of control with your next food choice. You are probably never going to have a craving for grilled chicken or a salad when your blood sugar is low; your body is smarter than that. Instead, pretzels, pizza, cookies, chips, fries, a granola bar, fruit, or rice will be calling your name. That's right, all the carbs you know and love! And it doesn't matter whether you're craving salty carbs such as potato chips or something sugary such as a doughnut; all carbs break down to sugar in the body.

So it's no mistake that you find yourself diving face-first into a bag of popcorn, chocolates, or crackers by noon, all the while thinking, "Why can I not stop eating these?" Our body craves these foods because it knows they will help pick our blood sugar back up quickly! It can almost feel like you have a little devil on one shoulder screaming for carbs, a lot louder than the angel on your other shoulder, who helps you think more rationally. But this isn't a little devil on your shoulder or even the real you talking; it's simply your blood sugar.

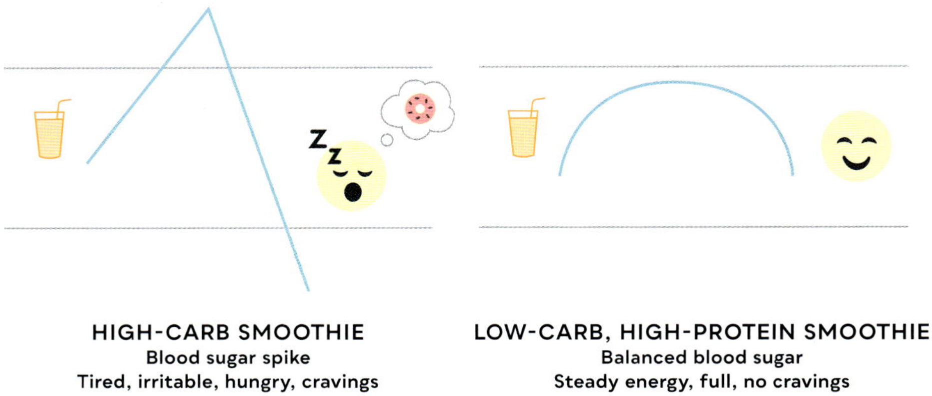

High-Protein, Low-Carbohydrate Smoothies

If we make a smoothie by prioritizing ingredients that don't break down to blood sugar, such as protein, fat, and fiber, instead of that high-sugar smoothie, our body responds differently. Let's say we choose one carbohydrate, such as half of a banana or even berries for a higher-fiber, lower-sugar option, to keep in the smoothie. We then switch the liquid to unsweetened nut milk and add a scoop of protein powder, some veggies, and 1 tablespoon (16 g) of peanut butter.

We have now created a balance of macronutrients that will help support our blood sugar. The protein from the protein powder, fat from the peanut butter, and fiber from the veggies will help to buffer the spike in blood sugar from the fruit, keeping everything nice and steady. So instead of feeling hangry soon after finishing your smoothie, you will feel chill, satiated, and energized. Not having those peaks and valleys in blood sugar can help keep you full for hours and in control at your next eating opportunity.

Blood Sugar and Weight

Blood sugar roller coasters can affect our weight in more ways than driving us to eat more food.

Hormones are our body's chemical messengers; they trigger different processes to occur in our body. Insulin, the hormone that rises after we eat, is responsible for telling the body what to do with the energy we just consumed. What you need to know is that our body is always shifting between being in a storage mode and being in a breakdown state, but it is always in predominantly one mode at a time. And these processes are dictated by, as you know, hormones!

It's kind of like the game tug-of-war—imagine that there are two sides fighting for control of your metabolic pathways. The captains of the two sides are our hormones: glucagon, the captain of the catabolic process, and insulin, the captain of the anabolic process.

On one side, the anabolic processes are in control, and your body is focused on storing things such as muscle mass and fat mass. And on the other side, the catabolic processes are in control, and your body prioritizes breaking the muscle and fat masses down. Because insulin is the captain of the anabolic processes, when it is elevated (or "winning"), it pushes our body into storage mode and prevents our body from burning fat. And guess what dictates these hormones? Our food! When we overproduce the hormone insulin after a high-carb, unbalanced meal, we are shifting our body out of fat-burning mode for a longer time, which is not ideal for weight loss.

Over time, a constant elevation in insulin can lead to insulin resistance. When someone has insulin resistance, it also means insulin is chronically elevated, which can make their ability to burn fat especially difficult. When we work with our hormones instead of against them, we can optimize our metabolism, which in this case can help us be more efficient at burning fat. Keeping blood sugar balanced can decrease the output of insulin, which can help to control cravings, prevent chronic illnesses, and manage weight.

When our blood sugar is outside of the normal range, it can affect how we metabolize our food, manage our cravings and hunger, and promote inflammatory responses, just to name a few reactions. In the short term, blood sugar dysregulation can make it hard for us to feel our best and to feel in control around food. In the long term, it can lead to chronic disease and weight gain. However, this unhealthy cycle can be changed, starting with portioning and balancing our carbohydrates with protein, fat, and fiber. When our blood sugar is in control, we feel in control! The mental and emotional drama around our food choices starts to vanish. We feel a sense of calm, satiety, and food freedom. And when we see the store-bought cookies someone brought to work on a random Tuesday, they won't tempt us nearly as much as they used to.

Carbohydrate Tolerance

Carbohydrates are our primary source of energy, meaning that when they are present, our body will always use them as its first fuel source. After carbohydrates have entered our bloodstream, we utilize the energy we need and the rest gets stored in our body. Most of the leftover carbohydrates get stored in our muscles as glycogen, which are basically strings of connected sugar molecules, and a smaller amount gets stored in our liver. Once those storage cabinets are filled up, any excess will be stored as fat because there is nowhere else for it to go. This is why the more active we are and the more muscle we have, the more carbohydrates we can tolerate. However, if we sit at a desk all day for work and on our bum all night watching TV, then our needs aren't as high as your favorite football player's might be.

Fructose Metabolism

We metabolize fructose, also known as fruit sugar, a little differently from how we metabolize glucose. All carbohydrates are composed of a mixture of simple sugars such as fructose, galactose, and/or glucose, but fructose is one of the types of sugar found naturally in fruit. You might have heard the name *fructose* in ingredients such as high-fructose corn syrup, which is a sweetener made from cornstarch that has a high concentration of fructose.

First and foremost, I want to make it super clear that fruit is highly nutritious for us and has many amazing benefits to our health. I would argue that many people should be replacing a lot of the refined carbohydrates they are consuming with high-fiber, whole foods–based carbohydrates such as fruit. However, despite what some nutrition programs may say, it doesn't make sense for fruit to be "unlimited" or "free." Fruit still breaks down to sugar, even if it is from a natural source. Because we are talking about smoothies—which make it so easy to blend many servings of fruit into one drink and consume it within minutes—I think this is especially worth chatting about.

Although the glucose from fruit will increase blood sugar, the fructose in fruit will metabolize a little differently. Fructose does not get absorbed into the bloodstream like glucose does. Instead, about 70 percent of the fructose we consume goes through our lymphatic system, which brings it straight to the liver. We can only metabolize and store so much fructose in the liver before our body starts to store it as fat.

Again, this isn't a concern when you're having a piece of fruit with your eggs for breakfast or a serving of berries in your protein smoothie. However, some smoothies have an excessive amount of fruit, fruit juices, and even natural sugars such as agave, and they have a much higher concentration of fructose. "Natural" sweeteners such as agave—which is about 80 percent fructose, by the way—have come out with health claims stating they are lower on the glycemic index. The glycemic index is a rating system that takes into account how rapidly a food can increase your blood sugar when you eat that food by itself. It has some merit, but don't be fooled by health trends such as agave, because its high-fructose content comes with its own host of problems.

Although fructose does not directly impact blood sugar, it can indirectly have an impact on the regulation of blood sugar. Excess fructose can lead to insulin resistance, and over time, insulin resistance impacts our ability to metabolize carbohydrates. High amounts of fructose in the diet can negatively impact cholesterol levels, blood pressure, blood sugar, insulin resistance, fatty liver disease, and weight over the long term.

A lot of my clients already intend to eat a pretty healthy diet but struggle with blood sugar control, cravings, insulin resistance, abnormal cholesterol levels, and weight loss. They eat a lot of nutritious foods such as fruits, but not in portions that work for their body. When we adjust their carbohydrate intake to their carbohydrate tolerance and adjust portions of foods such as fruit, they start to see improvements in their cholesterol levels, blood sugar, and insulin levels, and they finally start seeing the number on their scale drop. All this is to say, adding a portion of fruit to your smoothies is great for you! But, keep in mind that just because something is good for you doesn't mean you can't overdo it.

The Power of Protein

Now that you understand why it is important to balance blood sugar and control carbohydrates, let's explore why protein is the macronutrient we should be prioritizing. Protein is found mainly in animal products such as eggs, fish, beef, poultry, dairy, and, for our smoothies, protein powder! Amino acids are the building blocks of protein, and every cell of the human body, including hormones, neurotransmitters, DNA, enzymes, and more, is made up of protein. So essentially, we are made up of protein, which is why it is extremely important to consume it. Just like we want to support the metabolic process of blood sugar balance by portioning and balancing carbohydrates, we want to support our body's ability to build cells and function optimally by giving it the building blocks it needs.

PROTEIN AND METABOLISM

For health, weight loss, and overall longevity, one of the most crucial benefits of protein is that it helps our body build and maintain muscle mass. This is especially the case if your goal is weight loss because muscle mass loss is typically inevitable to some extent during weight loss. However, research shows that when we consume enough protein, we can hold on to more lean muscle mass while losing fat, leading to a more ideal body composition. The more muscle mass we have, the higher our metabolic rate is, meaning we burn more calories even when we are sitting on the couch watching our favorite Netflix show!

Because muscles are one of the main storage tanks for blood sugar, the more we improve our body composition and increase lean muscle mass, the better we can store, utilize, and metabolize carbs. This muscle mass helps to suck up excess blood sugar from the bloodstream like a vacuum, assisting with blood sugar regulation, and I think by now you are well aware of the benefits of that. In addition to all this good news, protein happens to also have the highest thermogenic effect of food. This means that we burn more calories breaking down and digesting protein than we do breaking down and digesting carbohydrates and fat. So we are essentially increasing our metabolism in multiple different ways when eating more protein. Cool, right?

PROTEIN AND HUNGER HORMONES

But wait, there's more! Protein is the most satiating macronutrient. Although balancing blood sugar is one way it helps to control appetite, there are other mechanisms involved as well. There is evidence to suggest that when we replace some carbohydrates with protein even when calories are controlled, we get greater satiety and satisfaction gained from meals as well as less blood sugar and insulin variability.

Protein helps to stimulate the release of certain hormones, including cholecystokinin, GLP-1, and PYY, which are hormones that slow down the digestion of our food and promote satiety. Protein also helps suppress ghrelin, a hunger hormone that stimulates appetite and actually reminds me a bit of a gremlin bugging you to eat. I don't know about you, but hunger is definitely the gremlin I'm always trying to fight off! We have nerves and sensors on our gut lining that respond to the amino acids from protein that we consume in our diet by releasing hunger hormones. These hormones then communicate with the brain via the gut-brain axis, as if they were on a corded telephone calling up to say, "Hey there, we're full! You can put the meatballs down now!"

The protein leverage hypothesis developed by Stephen Simpson and David Raubenheimer suggests that despite the energy or calorie content of food, we will continue to eat until our protein needs are met; that means we may overconsume carbohydrates and fats until we have received a

Protein at Breakfast

Roller coasters at an amusement park might be fun, but internal ones . . . not so much. Although a lack of protein in general can impact hunger, breaking your fast with a high-carb, low-protein smoothie triggers a blood sugar roller coaster that will guarantee cravings and enhanced hunger all day long. If you don't like that ride, you can change the course. Research shows that lack of protein at breakfast leads to cravings for carbs later in the day. With the right amount of protein in your smoothie, you'll notice cravings decrease as you actually feel full, satisfied, and energized, all the while losing weight. These little tweaks honestly make a huge impact!

To put things simply, a high-protein diet is ideal for maintaining and building muscle mass, improving muscle composition, increasing metabolism, suppressing appetite, and even helping to prevent weight regain after weight loss. It helps us feel more satisfied and satiated throughout the day, which positively influences our future food choices, making weight management a lot easier. This is why prioritizing protein at meals is key if you want to boost your metabolism and have fewer obsessive thoughts about food while getting toned.

certain number of amino acids from our food. So, if you feel like you have no off button with certain foods, there's a good chance that prioritizing protein will help.

Counting Carbs Over Calories

My smoothies are not the typical low-calorie smoothies known to set off hunger and cravings again by the time you finish reading this sentence. Often, we think of *healthy* or *weight loss–friendly* as eating fewer calories and the least amount of fat possible. But if this concept really works, why is our population more overweight and sicker than ever? Although I don't think it is necessary to meticulously count the total number of carbohydrates in your smoothie, keeping an eye on and counting those portions for starch and sugar is key. In the next chapter, we will dive deeper into what that will look like. But first, let's talk about why focusing on just calorie counts isn't helping us.

Composition Matters!

Although a lot of people preach that it's all about "calories in, calories out," newer research is showing us otherwise. Calories are not created equal; what our food is made up of matters. Low-calorie, high-carb, low-protein food choices trigger cravings for more food at other points in our day. Despite our good intentions or "willpower," biology will eventually take over. And biology always wins. In reality, that 200-calorie breakfast smoothie actually drives you to eat more food throughout the day because it does not regulate your hunger. Even when the smoothies we drink or foods we eat have the same calorie count, the composition matters.

A study by Belinda Lennerz et al. showed that when study participants consumed a 500-calorie high-glycemic meal, the hunger and craving region of their brain was activated significantly more than it was when they consumed a 500-calorie low-glycemic meal. Simply put, the high-glycemic meal drove them to want to eat more later on. If you want to turn off hunger, focus on meal replacements that optimize your metabolism to eliminate the feeling of being hormonally driven by food all the time.

When Should You Drink Your Smoothie?

The smoothies in this book, aside from the ones in the snack chapter, are designed to be meal replacements. My smoothie formula is designed to be a complete meal, so you can enjoy it any time of day. However, the great thing about having your smoothie for breakfast is that it's easy, quick, and great for those on the go. It's one less thing you have to think about in the morning if you want to have a consistent healthy option to set you up for success! They are also a good option for anyone who isn't used to eating in the morning because they are nourishing and filling enough to be a meal, but they don't sit as heavily in your stomach as solid food does.

2

MY LOW-CARB SMOOTHIE FORMULA

AS I HOPE YOU'VE LEARNED BY NOW, a healthy smoothie's creation goes beyond aimlessly adding fruits and vegetables to a blender and calling it a meal or a snack. My original smoothie formula is a guideline for creating a balanced, low-carb smoothie! It is designed to give you the nourishment you need to stay full for hours, minimize cravings, and power through your day feeling energized. All you need to do is balance your portions of protein, fat, and fiber.

Just like when you bake a cake, following a recipe for a smoothie will ensure quality and consistency. My formula is my recipe for balanced nutrition. All the smoothies found in this book are assembled using this formula, but I also encourage you to try out your own creations by simply mixing and matching ingredients for each component of the formula.

Now let's give your smoothies a makeover!

Low-Carb Smoothie Formula

- → Protein: 20–35 grams
- → Fat: 1–2 servings (10–25 grams)
- → Fiber: 6+ grams
    - ⊕ Veggies: unlimited
    - ⊕ Fruit: 1 serving or about ½ cup
    - ⊕ Added fiber: 1–2 tablespoons (12–25 g*) fiber powder

      *In this case, grams is referring to the *weight* of the fiber source, not the actual amount of fiber in the tablespoons.
- → Low-carb liquids: 1–2 cups (237-473 ml)
- → Boosts (*optional*): to taste

Prioritize Protein

Protein is an essential part of a balanced meal. As I've said before, it helps to stabilize blood sugar, maintain and build muscle mass, and keep metabolism up. Out of all the macronutrients, protein has the highest thermogenic effect, meaning it takes more calories to break down protein than it does to break down carbohydrates or fat. Because protein is the most satiating macronutrient, it is most directly responsible for efficiently shutting down food cravings, especially for carbs! If you are looking to optimize your health and/or shed fat while staying full, aim for 20 to 35 grams of protein per smoothie. If you are struggling with insulin resistance or diabetes or if you are doing an extensive workout program, I highly suggest aiming for 30 grams minimum.

WHAT'S THE DEAL WITH PROTEIN POWDER?

Most people think protein powder is a supplement that automatically makes you bulky, reserved for bodybuilders. However, that's not the case. Protein powder should be considered as simply another protein source, like chicken, fish, beef, and eggs. Protein powders are a great way to meet your smoothie's protein needs and to add flavor and sweetness while not overdoing the carbohydrates or fat. Finding a protein powder you love is important because it can really make or break the taste and texture of your smoothie. If you're not a fan of protein powder, you can replace it with plain Greek yogurt, cottage cheese, or even organic tofu. That said, these substitutes are not naturally sweet, so you may need to add a natural sugar replacement to adjust the sweetness to your liking.

All protein powders are not created equal, and especially if you will be using a protein powder on a regular basis, quality is important. Pick the best protein powder for your lifestyle and preferences with the tips below.

How to Pick a Protein Powder

On the nutrition facts label, you want to look for the following:

- → At least 20 grams of protein per serving
- → Less than 5 grams net carbs (This is a protein powder, not a carbohydrate powder! See the sidebar on net carbohydrates on page 21)
- → Six ingredients or fewer (it should ideally just be the protein source, flavoring such as vanilla or cocoa, and a sweetener)
- → A natural sugar substitute such as stevia, monk fruit, or erythritol for sweetening

Types of Protein Powders

There are many different types of protein powders to choose from, so I created the chart on the following page to help you pick the best option for you!

Protein Powder	Pros	Cons
Whey	Highly researched, most bioavailable, contains all essential amino acids, 99% lactose-free, tends to taste the best, made using a chemical-free process	Not suitable for those with a dairy sensitivity or allergy
Pea	Plant-based, dairy-free, vegan-friendly	Can sometimes be higher carb/lower protein per serving, less bioavailable, more likely to contain heavy metals, some people find it chalky, usually made with the chemical hexane
Bone broth	Contains glycine, glutamine, and cysteine, which help make a powerful amino acid and antioxidant, glutathione; great for repairing the gut barrier, dairy-free, made using a chemical-free process	Can be harder to find
Beef	Great source of essential amino acids, branched-chain amino acids, and collagen; made using a chemical-free process	Can be harder to find, may not be great for those with histamine intolerance
Collagen	Most abundant protein in our body; supports tissue repair for joints, tendons, ligaments, hair, skin, and nails; dairy-free; supports gut health; great for adding additional protein to your smoothie	Not a complete protein, doesn't contain essential amino acids, can be less satiating, not recommended as the primary protein in a smoothie

Tip When you go to look for a protein powder, you will see tons of different flavors to choose from. To keep things simple, most of the smoothie recipes in this book call for either a vanilla protein powder or a chocolate protein powder, with just a few calling for unflavored protein powder to keep their other flavors as accurate as possible. If you have to pick only one flavor of protein powder to purchase, I suggest vanilla. It can give your smoothie a nice, mild, sweet flavor and it is versatile. To make it chocolate, just add some cacao powder to your smoothie!

Net Carbohydrates

When picking a protein powder, you want to look at the net carbohydrates, not the total carbohydrates. Net carbohydrates is the total amount of carbohydrates digested from a food. Because our body does not actually digest fiber or sugar alcohol, we don't have to count them toward the total carbohydrate amount. When reading a nutrition facts label, you can calculate the net carbohydrates with this equation: **total carbohydrates minus fiber and sugar alcohols.**

Note that a product will not have sugar alcohols on the nutrition facts label unless the product has sugar alcohols in it. If the product does contain sugar alcohols, you will see it under the Carbohydrates portion of the nutrition facts labels, listed either as sugar alcohol or by the specific name of the sugar alcohol itself (e.g., erythritol, maltitol, or sorbitol). I suggest sticking to erythritol as your only sugar alcohol because it can be naturally derived and is considered to be the most well tolerated.

Nutrition Facts

Serving size	1 Scoop (43g)
Amount Per Serving	
Calories	**120**
	% Daily Value*
Total Fat 2g	**3%**
Saturated Fat 0.5g	**3%**
Trans Fat 0g	
Cholesterol 0mg	**0%**
Sodium 150mg	**7%**
Total Carbohydrate 17g	**6%**
Dietary Fiber 7g	**25%**
Total Sugars 1g	
Includes 0g Added Sugars	
Sugar Alcohol 8g	
Protein 20g	**35%**
Vitamin D 0mcg	0%
Calcium 97mg	8%
Iron 4mg	20%
Potassium 200mg	4%

*The % Daily Value (DV) tells you how much a nutrient in a serving of food contributes to a daily diet. 2,000 calories a day is used for general nutrition advice.

Here is an example of a nutrition facts label for net carbohydrates.

Net Carbohydrates

Total carbohydrates: 17g

- fiber: 7g

- sugar alcohol: 8g

= net carbs: 2g

Collagen Protein Powders

Collagen is the most abundant protein in our body. It is made up primarily of the amino acids proline, glycine, and hydroxyproline. Our body does create its own collagen; however, when we are under stress and when we age, our production of collagen starts to decline. Supporting our bodies' natural production of collagen with a collagen supplement can be helpful for our gut health, hair, skin, nails, and joints.

Still, it's important to consider that collagen is an incomplete protein, meaning it does not have all the essential amino acids. Collagen is okay to use as a protein source if you eat animal proteins at other meals, because you will get all your essential amino acids from those sources. However, collagen is a thinner protein and will not make your smoothie as thick as other protein powders will. This, in addition to the lack of some essential amino acids, may make your smoothie less filling than it would be if you used other protein sources.

One of the best ways to use collagen, especially if you are aiming for 30 to 35 grams of protein in your smoothie or trying to reap the benefits of collagen, is to combine it with another protein powder. There are a lot of flavorless collagen options that will not affect your smoothie's texture or taste, and one serving will add a nice boost of protein (about 10 grams) to your smoothie!

Fat Is Your Friend

Just like protein, fat is an essential macronutrient found in every cell in our body. Nuts, seeds, coconut, avocado, and healthy oils are all great sources of fat that help to reduce inflammation as well as balance hormones and blood sugar. Fat regulates hunger hormones and slows down the digestion of your meal, keeping you full for longer. Adding fat to your smoothie will help with the flavor and satisfaction factor, all the while lowering your overall carbohydrates. However, despite what the keto police may say, our low-carb smoothies are not unlimited in fat; portion control is still important. Aiming for 1 to 2 servings or 10 to 25 grams of fat per smoothie is a great guideline to make sure you're reaping the benefits of those healthy fats without overdoing it.

Be Carb Conscious, Not Carb Obsessed

Although this smoothie formula is low carb, it's not zero carb. There's a huge misconception that less is better so none is the best, but that's not true. Carbs are great for getting energy, fiber, and certain nutrients; however, portion control and balancing your carbs with protein, fat, and fiber are key to getting the most out of your smoothies!

Stay Full with Fiber

Fiber is the nondigestible part of carbohydrates. Besides the other amazing benefits we get from fiber, such as supporting the immune system, keeping digestion regular, and keeping the heart healthy, fiber will help keep us full—another important component of a smoothie. Because we don't digest fiber, it helps slow the release of carbohydrates into our bloodstream. This keeps blood sugar levels stable and hunger in check. Fiber also adds volume and weight to our smoothie, which helps make us feel full. As previously mentioned, the smoothie formula is low carb, not zero carb. We want most of the carbohydrates in our smoothie to come from fiber so we can reap its benefits without spiking our blood sugar.

Fiber is the umbrella category of the carbohydrate components of our smoothie; the carbs and fiber in our smoothies will be coming from veggies, added fiber sources, and/or some fruit. Instead of focusing on lowering carbohydrates, I highly suggest prioritizing fiber. Choose at least one—or all three—of these fiber sources to put in your smoothie. The choice is yours, but the more fiber, the more filling!

VOLUMIZE YOUR VEGGIES

The best part about veggies in smoothies is that you usually don't taste them (unless you're really trying to, like with the Carrot Cake Smoothie!). My favorite veggies to add to smoothies are frozen cauliflower and frozen summer squash because they make the smoothie cold and creamy. It's like having ice in your smoothie but without watering it down or changing the flavor! You can also do a handful of greens such as spinach or kale, which are loaded with antioxidants, phytochemicals, vitamins, and minerals and are even associated with slower cognitive decline. However, keep in mind that they will not provide as much fiber or bulk as cauliflower or squash do, and that bulk helps keep us full. So if you are really trying to promote satiety, pairing greens with one of the other options may be ideal.

Sugar Misconceptions

Not many people would sit down and eat a banana, a cup of pineapple, a cup of berries, and a pear, only to wash it down with a glass of juice in a single sitting. Yet, people will blend those ingredients up and drink it within seconds! In a smoothie, where you can effortlessly pulverize anything into an easily drinkable form, the sugar content can become quite high. Ideally, we want the sugar we do consume to come from a natural source such as fruit. Still, despite being natural, that sugar piles up and can negatively impact our long-term health.

At the end of the day, all carbs (besides fiber) break down to sugar, so pay attention to the total carb amount, not just the sugar content. Yes, fruit is healthy and we should absolutely enjoy it—just in portions! That's why, with the help of my low-carb smoothie formula, you will know how to incorporate the proper portions of fruit into your smoothie.

Veggies are optional in a smoothie, but I highly recommend them. Aim for about 1 cup (237 ml) in your smoothie—although there's no such thing as too many veggies!

HAVE FUN WITH FRUIT (BUT NOT TOO MUCH FUN!)

Unlike most smoothies online and at your local smoothie bar, the smoothies you can make with this book are designed to keep sugar to a minimum and to feature natural sources of sugar such as fruit. The last thing I want is for you to have a sugar bomb first thing in the morning and then crash 90 minutes later, feeling lethargic and hungry again. Instead, I want you to feel fueled, satiated, and energized throughout your day! Fruit is a great way to add flavor and some nutrients to your smoothie. Just make sure to stick to a portion size that will help you keep blood sugar balanced and cravings at bay! For a low-carb smoothie, keep fruit to an optional one serving, which is about ½ cup (118 ml) for most fruits. Because berries are very high in fiber and lower in sugar, you can go up to 1 cup (237 ml).

ADDED FIBER

Daily fiber recommendations for men are 30 to 38 grams per day and for women are 21 to 25 grams per day. However, most people don't get even half of their recommended fiber intake. It's especially lacking when people start implementing a low-carb lifestyle and cut out all the carbs in their diet instead of just prioritizing fiber. Along with veggies and fruit, added fiber options such as chia seeds, flaxseeds, psyllium husk, and inulin powder are a great way to pack an extra punch of fiber into your day. You can easily get almost half your daily fiber needs in your smoothie if you bulk it up with veggies, a serving of high-fiber fruit, and a fiber powder.

These fibers are optional in all recipes. When adding fiber to your diet, especially when it is from a more concentrated source, start slow and see how you tolerate it. Although I typically call for 1 tablespoon (12 g) of fiber for a smoothie, feel free to start with 1 to 2 teaspoons, especially if using inulin, and work your way up to 1 tablespoon from there.

The following chart can help you find the right fiber option! For example, if you are trying to lose weight and are closer to your goal weight, it may be ideal to use the options that are lower in fat because you already get the fat in your smoothies from other sources. If you struggle with abnormal cholesterol levels, psyllium husk could be a great option to help naturally improve your levels. If you don't like smoothies super thick, inulin might be your favorite go-to! Always ask your doctor before taking any supplement and make sure to check whether there are any interactions that could negatively conflict with medication you take.

Fibers	Grams of Fiber per Tablespoon	Other Benefits	Fat Content	Smoothie Thickness
Chia seeds	~4	Contains omega-3 fatty acids, magnesium, copper, thiamine, and protein	High	Very thick
Psyllium husk	~3.5	Highly researched for improving cholesterol levels	Low	Very thick
Flaxseed	~2.8	Contains omega-3 fatty acids, magnesium, copper, selenium, and protein	High	Medium thickness
Inulin powder	~2.5	Dissolves easily; mild, sweet flavor	Low	Mild thickness

BOOSTS

Boosts are ingredients you can add to your smoothie that provide little to no caloric value, but can enhance the flavor or nutritional value of your smoothie. For example, cacao powder, cinnamon, maca powder, and matcha powder can help load your smoothies with beneficial compounds such as antioxidants, vitamins, minerals, and phytochemicals, all the while providing delicious flavors. Extracts are another example of a flavor enhancer that can add a twist of flavor to your vanilla or chocolate base.

Having a consistent meal option such as a smoothie each day can really make your health journey so much easier! Lean on something you know will make you feel great, nourish your body, and give you one fewer decision to make each day—it can only help with overall consistency in this hectic world we live in. However, you don't want to get bored. As they say, variety is the spice of life. With limitless smoothie flavor options using my formula, you can have fun playing around with these boosts to keep your smoothies fun and exciting!

LOW-CARB LIQUIDS

Choosing a liquid for your smoothie can be tricky with so many different healthy alternatives out there. Many people are leaning on oat milk for a healthier, dairy-free milk alternative; however, from a blood-sugar and health standpoint, this is just not a trend I can get behind. Each 8-ounce (237 ml) glass of oat milk has around 15 grams of carbohydrates, which is equivalent to a slice of bread or a carb serving. Most people will be putting almost 2 cups (473 ml) of liquids in their smoothie, so double that. That's a lot of unnecessary carbohydrates! You would be much better off using fruit as your carbohydrate because it is wrapped in fiber and slower to digest, keeping blood sugar more stable. Honestly, especially because oat milk does not contribute much flavor to your smoothie, it is usually not worth using.

When choosing a liquid for your smoothie, make sure it is not only low in sugar but also low in total carbs. Remember, all carbs besides fiber break down to sugar in the body. When these carbs are in liquid form, they digest particularly quickly, which has a steeper impact on blood sugar.

Some nut-based milks are higher in fat than others. If your goal is weight loss and you choose a nut-based milk that is more concentrated, meaning over 5 grams fat per serving, I suggest decreasing the fat you are using in your smoothie or diluting the milk with water. Diluting will still bring creaminess to your smoothie while keeping your portions in check. My top recommendations for smoothies are water, unsweetened nut milks, seed milks, and coconut milk (not from a can; when we use the coconut milk from a can, it is more concentrated in fat, so we count it as fat).

Tip You can adjust your smoothie's thickness to your preference. If you prefer a thinner smoothie, you can use more liquid, and if you prefer a thicker smoothie, you can use less liquid. I find that between 1 cup (237 ml) and 2 cups (473 ml) of liquid is suitable for most people, but I encourage you to experiment and see what end of that range you enjoy most. As you start making smoothies, take note of the thickness you appreciate so you can adjust the liquid amount in your future attempts. Keep in mind that certain ingredients, such as added fiber and avocado, will really thicken your smoothie, so in smoothies that are made up of those ingredients, you might want a little more liquid than you normally would use.

NATURAL SUGAR SUBSTITUTES

It's important to understand that even though more natural sugars such as maple syrup, date syrup, agave, and honey might be packed with some health benefits, such as vitamins, minerals, and antioxidants, the body is going to respond to them in the same way it does to refined sugar. One tablespoon of these sugars has about 16 grams of carbohydrates, which is equivalent to a slice of bread. It's easy for them to add up! That's not to say you should never use these sugars; however, portions are key. In a smoothie specifically, you're better off getting your sweetness from fruit, protein powder, or a natural sugar alternative.

Although I am also not a fan of artificial sugars, there are some great natural sugar substitutes you can use to sweeten your smoothies without adding extra carbohydrates or calories. These include pure stevia, monk fruit, and erythritol. I recommend avoiding most sugar alcohols, but erythritol can be naturally derived and is typically well tolerated, so I do recommend it.

These natural sugar substitutes are a great way to adjust your smoothie's sweetness to your taste while still keeping them low carb.

Swaps

The flexibility of my low-carb smoothie formula makes it easy to use. Although flavor profiles were tested using the specific ingredients listed for each recipe, you can always make swaps as needed with what you have in your fridge, freezer, or pantry. Feel free to swap any ingredient

HOW TO BUILD YOUR SMOOTHIE

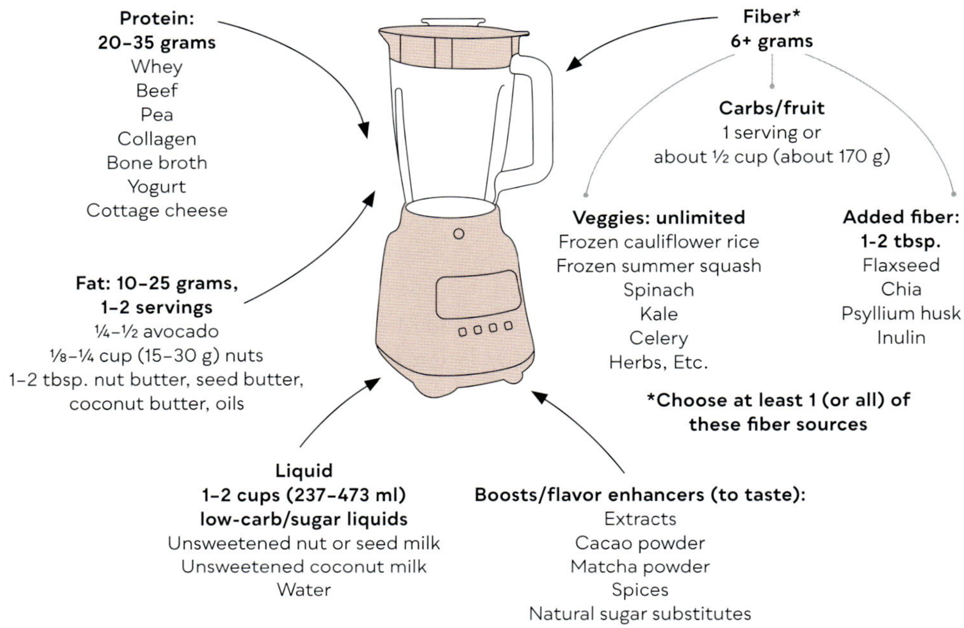

with another from that specific food group. For example, you don't have almond butter for your fat source? Go ahead and swap for another nut butter such as cashew butter or a serving of almonds instead! Don't have strawberries for your fruit? Feel free to use raspberries or another fruit of your choice! Even though this might slightly alter the flavor of your smoothie profile, it will still be pretty close—and, I'm sure, equally delicious!

Below are some examples of swaps that can be helpful for keeping the flavor profile close to the original recipe:

→ Swapping any nut butter for another or for a serving of nuts is a great option. Keep in mind that peanut butter does have a strong flavor, so if you do not want to taste peanut butter, almond butter and cashew butter are milder options.

→ Avocado and coconut milk or cream from a can are both pretty mild in flavor, so it's easy to swap for one another. Just remember that avocado will make your smoothie a little thicker than coconut, and, of course, it will make it greener too!

- → Any of the added fibers are interchangeable with one another. I'd recommend checking the chart on page 25 to see how different options might affect smoothie thickness.
- → Any liquid choices are easily interchangeable with one another. Unsweetened coconut milk has a strong flavor compared with most of the milk choices out there; however, unsweetened nut or seed milks typically are pretty mild in flavor.
- → You can swap frozen veggies such as cauliflower rice, zucchini, and yellow squash with one another throughout the book. Use what you like or just what you have on hand. They are basically tasteless in smoothies and interchangeable with one another. The main reason they were chosen in certain recipes was simply to keep the traditional color of the smoothie. Still, when it comes to veggies, as long as you've got them, you can't go wrong!

Juicing Versus Smoothies

A juice might look similar to a smoothie, but in reality they are two totally different beverages. That's especially true when the smoothie in question is made by following my low-carb smoothie formula!

When we juice a fruit or vegetable, we remove the fiber and leave the sugar on its own. But as I've been shouting from the rooftops, fiber is important to our health and satiety. It is where most of our carbohydrates should be coming from. When we strip the fiber away and drink what's left of the produce—which, may I remind you, is mostly sugar—it digests rapidly, spiking our blood sugar and leaving our stomach empty and our hunger hormones screaming at us to eat an hour later. Especially with no protein, fat, or fiber to act as a buffer for these predigested carbohydrates, the fiber-free sugars force us on a blood-sugar roller coaster that over time can lead to weight gain, diabetes and inflammation.

Of course, one juice here and there is not going to be harmful to your health; it just won't be helpful either. Most people trying to incorporate juices into their day are trying to improve their health and drink them too often, sometimes for every meal or for days on end if they're doing a "juice cleanse." In situations like this, juice is really doing more harm than good. Keeping the fiber attached to your produce and pairing it with protein and fat will make all the difference for your health, energy, and waistline.

Smoothie Meal Prep

Smoothies are an easy, convenient option for having a healthy meal that will help keep you in balance and full for hours. You can stock your pantry and freezer with all the essentials so you always have ingredients on hand, and you'll be able to whip up a meal in a matter of minutes. Here are some smoothie meal prep tips.

First, you can always make your smoothie the day before you want to eat it and keep it in your fridge so that it's ready to go. If you do this, skip the added fiber in your smoothie, because if added fibers sit for too long, they will make your smoothie extremely thick and hard to drink.

SMOOTHIE FREEZER PACKS

It's always a good idea to keep a few smoothie freezer packs in your freezer in case you need a backup on a busy morning. To make these, all you need to do is combine all the ingredients you would put in your smoothie (except the liquid) into a small container or silicon bag and keep in the freezer until you're ready for your smoothie. Then when you're looking for a quick and nourishing meal, place the contents of the freezer bag into your blender with your low-carb liquid of choice.

SMOOTHIE ICE CUBES

You can premake your smoothie and then pour the blend into ice cube trays. When you're ready to have your smoothie, all you have to do is pop the ice cubes into your blender, throw in a little extra liquid of your choice, and blend away!

Adjusting Your Smoothies

The smoothie formula presented in this chapter is a flexible guideline that allows for wiggle room so you can tweak for your individual taste buds and needs. Use these guidelines to help you figure out what ratio works best for you. The goal is to stay full for at least four hours after drinking a smoothie, prevent mindless snacking, and give your body the tools it needs to function optimally. I encourage you to pay attention to what ingredients and recipes have you feeling your best. What ends of the spectrums for the macronutrient ranges help you achieve your goals? Do you feel better without fruit in your smoothie? Or maybe you're less tempted by the snacks in your pantry when you have 30 grams of protein instead of 20 grams? Pay attention to these little details because they, along with the formula, should help guide your food choices. It's always important to adjust to what is showing to be ideal for you and your bio individuality.

3

THE CLASSICS

Let's start off strong with low-carb, high-protein versions of some of the smoothie world's most popular flavors! Whether you're a peanut butter and chocolate lover or more of a green smoothie enthusiast, I have a recipe for you. This is an especially great chapter to dive into if you are newer to smoothies. These simple yet delicious flavor profiles will have your taste buds enjoying flavors you love while your belly is kept full for hours on end!

Chocolate Peanut Butter Cup

If you're a chocolate–peanut butter fan like I am, this might become one of your go-to recipes! Enjoy this classic flavor combo, which will make you feel like you're drinking one of your favorite desserts for a meal.

YIELD: 1 SMOOTHIE

INGREDIENTS

1 serving chocolate protein powder
1½ tablespoons (24 g) peanut butter
1 tablespoon (5 g) cacao powder
1 tablespoon (5 g) psyllium husk
1 cup (114 g) cauliflower rice, frozen
pinch sea salt
1½ cups (355 ml) unsweetened almond milk

DIRECTIONS

Place all ingredients in a blender and blend on high until smooth. Serve.

Green Goddess

When I'm trying to feel like a healthy badass who takes care of herself, but I still want something sweet and tasty, this is what I blend up. The mild vanilla flavor of the protein powder combined with the creaminess from the avocado, the sweetness from the banana, and the zest of the lemon cuts through the taste of the greens and makes for an excellent green smoothie.

YIELD: 1 SMOOTHIE

INGREDIENTS

1 serving vanilla protein powder
½ avocado
½ cup (125 g) frozen spinach
½ frozen banana
juice of ½ small lemon
1 tablespoon (13 g) ground flaxseed
2 cups (473 ml) unsweetened coconut milk

DIRECTIONS

Place all ingredients in a blender and blend on high until smooth. Serve.

Fun Fact

Leafy greens such as spinach have a sugar molecule that contains sulfur, which feeds the good bacteria in our gut.

Strawberry Banana

This timeless creation is the perfect blend of strawberry and banana. It's a low-carb, high-protein twist on an oldie but goodie. This thick, creamy smoothie is a yummy, fruity meal that will keep cravings away and hunger at bay.

YIELD: 1 SMOOTHIE

INGREDIENTS

1 serving vanilla protein powder
1 tablespoon (16 g) cashew butter
2 teaspoons inulin
⅓ cup (47 g) frozen strawberries
⅓ frozen banana
1 cup (114 g) cauliflower rice, frozen
1½ cups (355 g) unsweetened almond milk

DIRECTIONS

Place all ingredients in a blender and blend on high until smooth. Serve.

Strawberry Banana (on left) and Very Berry (on right; recipe on page 36)

Very Berry

I gotta say, I am berry *happy with how this smoothie tastes. The different berries blend flawlessly together to create a sweet, mildly tart flavor.*

YIELD: 1 SMOOTHIE

INGREDIENTS

1 serving vanilla protein powder
1 tablespoon (13 g) ground flaxseed
¼ cup (35 g) frozen strawberries
¼ cup (35 g) frozen blueberries
¼ cup (37 g) frozen raspberries
2 tablespoons (30 ml) canned coconut cream
1½ cups (355 ml) unsweetened almond milk

DIRECTIONS

Place all ingredients in a blender and blend on high until smooth. Serve.

NOTE Feel free to swap out the berries for whatever berries you enjoy most!

Double Chocolate Sea Salt

This decadent and classic chocolate smoothie flavor is sure to satisfy your chocolate cravings. Plus, who doesn't love a little sweet and salty combo? Definitely give this recipe a try if you want a chocolate fix without the sugar crash afterward.

YIELD: 1 SMOOTHIE

INGREDIENTS

1 serving chocolate protein powder
1 tablespoon (5 g) cacao powder
1 tablespoon (16 g) almond butter
1 tablespoon (8 g) chia seeds
1 cup (152 g) zucchini, frozen
pinch sea salt, plus another pinch for topping
1½ cups (355 ml) unsweetened almond milk

DIRECTIONS

Place all ingredients in a blender and blend on high until smooth.

Pour smoothie into a glass and top with another pinch of sea salt. Serve.

TIP If you cannot find frozen zucchini, you can buy raw zucchini (or yellow squash), cut it up into cubes uncooked, and freeze for smoothies!

Avocado Mint Chip

The first time I drank this avocado mint chip smoothie, it immediately brought me back to my early college years. I wasn't a huge mint chip fan at the time, but I actually grew a love for it because my boyfriend (now fiancé) was always eating it. I used to sneak bites of it and slowly started to really develop a taste for it. The fresh mint and avocado in this recipe make this smoothie a refreshing, creamy twist on an all-time favorite ice cream flavor.

YIELD: 1 SMOOTHIE

INGREDIENTS

1 serving vanilla protein powder
¼ avocado
25 mint leaves, plus more to taste
1 cup (152 g) zucchini, frozen
1½ cups (355 ml) almond milk
2 tablespoons (30 g) cacao nibs or (30 g) sugar-free chocolate chips

DIRECTIONS

Place all ingredients except cacao nibs in a blender and blend on high until smooth.

Add cacao nibs and pulse for 15 seconds. Serve.

NOTE Despite the name of this recipe, the avocado is actually totally optional. If you're not an avocado fan, I am not sure we can be friends (just kidding!), but feel free to skip this ingredient. There is already plenty of fat coming from the chocolate. If you are a fan of bitter flavors, the cacao nibs could be a good choice for you, but if you prefer things pretty sweet, go with the sugar-free chocolate chips instead.

Peanut Butter Party

I'm not sure this smoothie recipe really needs much of a description. I mean, it's a peanut butter party! Have I not said enough? For my peanut butter fans, this is going to be the classic you will probably always go back to.

YIELD: 1 SMOOTHIE

INGREDIENTS

1 serving vanilla protein powder
1½ tablespoons (24 g) peanut butter
1 tablespoon (13 g) ground flaxseed
1 cup (114 g) cauliflower rice, frozen
pinch sea salt
1 cup (237 ml) unsweetened almond milk

DIRECTIONS

Place all ingredients in a blender and blend on high until smooth. Serve.

NOTE If you have a peanut allergy or you don't like peanut butter for some odd reason, feel free to swap this ingredient with another nut or seed butter of your choice. Some great alternatives are almond butter, tahini, sunflower butter, walnut butter, and cashew butter. Whatever flavor palate you enjoy, there's a party for you to go to!

Pistachio Dream

I can't be the only one who used to spend hours on end deshelling and eating pistachios, right? Well, if you want that rewarding taste without the time sink, try this smoothie.

YIELD: 1 SMOOTHIE

INGREDIENTS

1 serving vanilla protein powder
¼ cup (31 g) unshelled and unsalted pistachios
1 tablespoon (5 g) psyllium husk
¼ cup (63 g) frozen spinach or small handful of fresh spinach
1 cup (152 g) zucchini, frozen
pinch sea salt
1½ cups (355 ml) unsweetened almond milk

DIRECTIONS

Place all ingredients in a blender and blend on high until smooth. Serve.

Mocha Pre-Workout

If you're not into fasted workouts, that's totally cool. You can still drink this before a super busy day. But if you do like to have something in your stomach before the gym, this is my favorite option. The MCT oil and coffee give the body a great source of energy for crushing a workout without adding in loads of sugar. It's my personal favorite when I need something before I go on a run.

YIELD: 1 SMOOTHIE

INGREDIENTS

1 serving chocolate protein powder
1 tablespoon (15 ml) MCT oil
2 teaspoons inulin
½ cup (57 g) cauliflower rice, frozen
1 cup (237 ml) coffee
1 cup (237 ml) unsweetened almond milk
natural sugar substitute to taste

DIRECTIONS

Place all ingredients in a blender and blend on high until smooth. Serve.

Fun Fact

MCT oil is made from a type of fat called medium-chain triglyceride, which gets absorbed differently than other types of fats we consume. Instead of going to the lymphatic system like the typical long-chain fats we eat, it goes straight to the bloodstream, where it can be used as a quick source of energy. It gives the body a fast energy source similar to carbohydrates without elevating blood sugar or insulin levels.

Peanut Butter Green Apple

Granny Smith apples dipped in peanut butter are one of my favorite food combinations. The crisp, sweet-yet-sour flavor of the green apple and the nuttiness of the peanut butter complement each other well. If this was one of your favorite snacks growing up, you have to give this recipe a try!

YIELD: 1 SMOOTHIE

INGREDIENTS

1 serving vanilla protein powder
1 tablespoon (16 g) peanut butter
1 small green apple
1 tablespoon (8 g) chia seeds
1 cup (152 g) zucchini, frozen
½ teaspoon vanilla extract
1½ cups (355 ml) unsweetened almond milk

DIRECTIONS

Place all ingredients in a blender and blend on high until smooth. Serve.

The Basic Green Smoothie

There's nothing wrong with being a little basic sometimes! Some things are staples for a good reason, right? This refreshing green smoothie will give you all the joy of a beautiful sunny day while making you look like you're keeping up with the trends.

YIELD: 1 SMOOTHIE

INGREDIENTS

1 serving vanilla protein powder
½ avocado
2 medium-size stalks of celery
½ cup (67 g) cubed cucumber
2 romaine leaves
1 green apple
juice of ½ lemon
½ cup (70 g) ice
1½ cups (355 ml) cold water

DIRECTIONS

Place all ingredients in a blender and blend on high until smooth. Serve.

NOTE Feel free to mix in any greens you'd like or that you have on hand. Bonus points for adding herbs such as parsley, cilantro, or mint! Herbs are anti-inflammatory, anticarcinogenic, and high in antioxidants, which helps support our overall health and reduce risk for chronic disease. Along with these benefits, herbs also have their own unique superpowers such as helping to support our bodies' natural detoxifying pathways or improving digestion issues!

4

SPRING SMOOTHIES

There is no better time to pull out your blender and whip up a smoothie than when spring is in the air! With the flowers starting to bud once again and the weather getting warmer, a cold, refreshing smoothie can really hit the spot. Enjoy these fruity, vibrant flavor choices that will have you looking and feeling your best, getting you all ready for a summer of fun.

Strawberry Rhubarb

Although rhubarb season falls short, the flavor in this smoothie does not! Rhubarb is a sour yet slightly sweet nonstarchy vegetable that pairs well with the sweet flavor of strawberries. If you have a chance to, head to your local farmers' market this spring or summer and pick up fresh rhubarb so you can try it in this recipe! Otherwise, you should be able to find it in the freezer section of grocery stores all year round.

YIELD: 1 SMOOTHIE

INGREDIENTS

1 serving vanilla protein powder
2 tablespoons (30 ml) canned coconut cream
1 cup (140 g) strawberries
1 cup (122 g) rhubarb
1½ cups (355 ml) unsweetened almond milk

DIRECTIONS

Place all ingredients in a blender and blend on high until smooth. Serve.

Coconut Blueberry Lemon Tart

Ready for a vacation, but your work schedule isn't? Feel the refreshing, divine taste of summer through this smoothie! This tropical, creamy combination is a tasty treat bursting with flavor.

YIELD: 1 SMOOTHIE

INGREDIENTS

1 serving vanilla protein powder
1 tablespoon (16 g) coconut butter
1 tablespoon (8 g) chia seeds
¾ cup (105 g) frozen wild blueberries
juice of ½ lemon
zest of ½ lemon
1½ cups (355 ml) unsweetened coconut milk
lemon zest to garnish

DIRECTIONS

Place all ingredients in a blender and blend on high until smooth. Serve.

NOTE Wild blueberries have twice as many antioxidants as regular blueberries do, and they have more fiber, too. You can find them in the frozen section of most grocery stores. However, if you don't have any wild blueberries on hand, regular blueberries will absolutely do!

Coconut Blueberry Lemon Tart (on left) and Lemon Cake (on right; recipe on page 50)

Lemon Cake

When life gives you lemons . . . you're gonna wanna make yourself this lemon cake smoothie! It's sweet, creamy, and zesty, just like all of the best lemon dishes and desserts are.

YIELD: 1 SMOOTHIE

INGREDIENTS

1 serving vanilla protein powder
1 tablespoon (16 g) cashew butter
juice of ½ lemon
½ teaspoon lemon zest
1 teaspoon vanilla extract
1 cup (114 g) cauliflower rice, frozen
1½ cups (355 ml) unsweetened almond milk

DIRECTIONS

Place all ingredients in a blender and blend on high until smooth. Serve.

Loaded Banana

This high-protein, low-carb beverage is really going to appeal to my banana lovers! You might even fall in (or slip into) love with this cold, creamy smoothie. Alongside banana, chocolate and peanut butter create an amazing flavor palette that, when combined, will be a total hit!

YIELD: 1 SMOOTHIE

INGREDIENTS

1 serving chocolate protein powder
1 teaspoon cacao powder
1 tablespoon (16 g) peanut butter
1 tablespoon (13 g) ground flaxseed
½ banana
1 cup (86 g) frozen cauliflower
1½ cups (355 ml) unsweetened coconut milk

DIRECTIONS

Place all ingredients in a blender and blend on high until smooth. Serve.

TIP For colder, creamier banana smoothies, peel and chop the bananas in advance and place them in the freezer for future smoothies. Remember to *remove the peel* before freezing!

Orange Creamsicle

Orange you glad I made this recipe? This smoothie has officially converted me to a creamsicle fan! The sweet and tart citrus flavors mixed here alongside the creamy texture is so satisfying for your taste buds and hunger.

YIELD: 1 SMOOTHIE

INGREDIENTS

1 serving vanilla protein powder
2 tablespoons (30 ml) canned coconut cream
1 tablespoon (5 g) psyllium husk
1 orange
1 cup (192 g) frozen yellow squash
1 teaspoon vanilla extract
½ teaspoon orange zest
1½ cups (355 ml) unsweetened almond milk

DIRECTIONS

Place all ingredients in a blender and blend on high until smooth. Serve.

Blueberry Pie

Blueberries are just little balls of bliss, aren't they? If you love blueberry pie, you'll like it even more without the sugar crash that often follows. This sippable dessert is truly a sweet, tasty treat.

YIELD: 1 SMOOTHIE

INGREDIENTS

1 serving vanilla protein
1 tablespoon (16 g) almond butter
1 tablespoon (13 g) ground flaxseed
½ cup (70 g) blueberries
1 cup (114 g) cauliflower rice, frozen
1 cup (237 ml) unsweetened almond milk

DIRECTIONS

Place all ingredients in a blender and blend on high until smooth. Serve.

NOTE Frozen foods get a bad rap, but often frozen produce is actually more nutritious than fresh. Fresh fruits and vegetables are usually picked before they are ripe, so their full nutrition potential hasn't fully developed yet. However, frozen produce is picked at its peak ripeness and then flash frozen to lock in all of its nutritious qualities until you are ready to eat them.

Strawberry Milkshake

My protein-packed milkshake brings all the muscles to the yard! And it brings a punch of flavor too. This creamy, fruity smoothie is perfect for cooling you off on a hot day and keeping the cravings away.

YIELD: 1 SMOOTHIE

INGREDIENTS

1 serving vanilla protein powder
1 tablespoon (16 g) cashew butter
½ cup (70 g) frozen strawberries
1 tablespoon (5 g) psyllium husk
1 cup (86 g) frozen cauliflower
½ teaspoon vanilla extract
pinch sea salt
1¼ cups (296 ml) unsweetened vanilla almond milk

DIRECTIONS

Place all ingredients in a blender and blend on high until smooth. Serve.

Matcha Mango Madness

Like many opposites, bitter and sweet come together to make something rich and deep in flavor. At different ends of the flavor spectrum, matcha and mango are two of my favorite tastes, and at risk of tooting my own horn, I've married them well in this smoothie!

YIELD: 1 SMOOTHIE

INGREDIENTS

1 serving vanilla protein powder
1 tablespoon (16 g) cashew butter
2 teaspoons inulin
1 tablespoon (6 g) matcha powder
½ cup (70 g) frozen mango chunks
1 cup (152 g) zucchini, frozen
1½ cups (355 ml) almond or coconut milk

DIRECTIONS

Place all ingredients in a blender and blend on high until smooth. Serve.

5

SUMMER SMOOTHIES

Smoothies are simply the perfect summertime meal! They're light, they're refreshing, and, best of all, they won't make you feel bloated when you put on your swimsuit. Plus, when it's hot and sunny outside, a cold, refreshing treat feels like the right way to start a day full of all the fun activities that summer can bring. In fact, setting the tone for your day with a meal that will keep you full for hours is going to help you tackle all the summertime craziness much more easily. But honestly, no matter what time of year it is, even if it's the dead of winter, these flavors will make you feel like you're lounging by a pool on a hot, sunny day. And I am personally always here for that!

Cocoa for Coconuts

This chocolate-coconut smoothie is the perfect mixture of fruity and decadent. These two superfoods are rich in both magnesium and taste! If you're a fan of this pair, you can't go wrong with this one.

YIELD: 1 SMOOTHIE

INGREDIENTS

1 serving chocolate protein powder
1 tablespoon (5 g) cacao powder
1 tablespoon (16 g) coconut butter
1 cup (152 g) zucchini, frozen
1 tablespoon (8 g) chia seeds
1½ cups (355 ml) unsweetened coconut milk

DIRECTIONS

Place all ingredients in a blender and blend on high until smooth. Serve.

Island Green

Most tropical smoothies are loaded with sugar. However, this one is simply loaded with protein, fat, fiber, and fun! This tropical treat will have you feeling super calm and chill as it turns off your hunger hormones. Kinda like how you'd feel if you were relaxing on an island beach, no?

YIELD: 1 SMOOTHIE

INGREDIENTS

1 serving vanilla protein powder
½ avocado
½ cup (32 g) frozen kale
¼ cup (35 g) frozen pineapple chunks
¼ cup (35 g) frozen mango
2 cups (473 ml) unsweetened almond or coconut milk

DIRECTIONS

Place all ingredients in a blender and blend on high until smooth. Serve.

Chocolate Cherry

Chocolate is already amazing on its own, but adding that touch of cherry takes it to the next level. Although frozen cherries will do the trick, I encourage you to take advantage of fresh cherries when they're in season for an extra-potent cherry flavor.

YIELD: 1 SMOOTHIE

INGREDIENTS

1 serving chocolate protein powder
2 tablespoons (30 ml) canned coconut cream
1 tablespoon (8 g) chia seeds
½ cup (88 g) frozen or fresh cherries, pitted
1 cup (152 g) zucchini, frozen
¼ teaspoon vanilla extract
1 cup (237 ml) unsweetened almond milk

DIRECTIONS

Place all ingredients in a blender and blend on high until smooth. Serve.

Tangy Blackberry Blast

Just like all calories aren't created equal, all yogurt options aren't created equal. Depending on which yogurt you pick up, it can be either really high in sugar and low in protein or vice versa. Choosing a plain Greek yogurt is going to be your best bet for the most nutritious and protein-packed choice. You can then sweeten it yourself, just as you do in this delicious smoothie recipe.

YIELD: 1 SMOOTHIE

INGREDIENTS

1 serving vanilla protein powder
1 tablespoon (16 g) cashew butter
½ cup (72 g) blackberries
½ cup (75 g) plain 2% Greek yogurt
1 cup (114 g) cauliflower rice, frozen
1½ cups (355 ml) unsweetened almond milk

DIRECTIONS

Place all ingredients in a blender and blend on high until smooth. Serve.

Pink Raspberry Lemonade

Lemon and raspberry are an underrated duo. This smoothie is sweet, tart, refreshing, and perfect for a hot sunny day. It also happens to be a prettier (and more filling!) twist on a classic beverage.

YIELD: 1 SMOOTHIE

INGREDIENTS

1 serving unflavored protein powder
1 tablespoon (15 ml) MCT oil
½ cup (70 g) frozen raspberries
juice of ½ lemon
1 tablespoon (8 g) chia seeds
natural sugar substitute to taste
1 cup (237 ml) cold water

DIRECTIONS

Place all ingredients in a blender and blend on high until smooth. Serve.

Tangy Blackberry Blast (on left; recipe on page 63) and Pink Raspberry Lemonade (on right)

Mango Turmeric

When a tropical fruit meets an exotic spice, this is what you get: a burst of flavor packed with a ton of nutrition that will keep you in good health. The benefits of this nutrient-packed smoothie will surprise you and your taste buds too!

YIELD: 1 SMOOTHIE

INGREDIENTS

1 serving vanilla protein powder
¼ cup (60 ml) canned coconut milk
½ cup (70 g) frozen mango chunks
1 tablespoon (13 g) ground flaxseed
½ teaspoon ground turmeric
pinch ground black pepper
1 cup (192 g) frozen yellow squash
1½ cups (355 ml) unsweetened almond milk

DIRECTIONS

Place all ingredients in a blender and blend on high until smooth. Serve.

TIP If you cannot find frozen yellow squash, just cut up some fresh yellow squash and put in the freezer uncooked for smoothies!

Chocolate and Greens

Remember when your mom always told you that you couldn't eat dessert until you ate your veggies? Well, show her this smoothie and prove that you can have it both ways! The chocolate-y deliciousness of this smoothie really masks the flavor of the greens. I bet you can't even taste them, even though you're getting all the benefits!

YIELD: 1 SMOOTHIE

INGREDIENTS

1 serving chocolate protein powder
1 tablespoon (5 g) cacao powder
¼ cup (28 g) chopped walnuts
½ cup (125 g) frozen spinach
½ cup (32 g) frozen kale
1½ cups (355 ml) unsweetened almond milk

DIRECTIONS

Place all ingredients in a blender and blend on high until smooth. Serve.

Fun Fact

Researchers found when looking at brain scans that people who consume one to two servings of leafy greens per day have brains that look eleven years younger!

Pink Dragon

This pretty-in-pink smoothie has a secret ingredient that creates its vibrant color—pink dragon fruit! Dragon fruit happens to be lower in sugar than most other tropical fruits, making it an ideal option for my fellow carb-conscious friends. The reddish-pink color in dragon fruit is due to the presence of the powerful antioxidant lycopene, which has also been linked to better heart health, brain health, and even better sleep quality. Because lycopene is a fat-soluble antioxidant, it is best paired with fat for better bioavailability, just like the coconut cream used in this smoothie.

YIELD: 1 SMOOTHIE

INGREDIENTS

1 serving vanilla protein powder
¾ cup (105 g) frozen pink dragon fruit
2 tablespoons (30 ml) canned coconut cream
1 tablespoon (8 g) chia seeds
1½ cups (355 ml) unsweetened coconut milk

DIRECTIONS

Place all ingredients in a blender and blend on high until smooth. Serve.

Fun Fact

Did you know dragon fruit is actually in the cactus family? If you have ever seen one, you might not be surprised that it is true. They're pretty funky-looking!

6

FALL SMOOTHIES

Fall is my favorite time of the year! Maybe it's because it's when my birthday is. Maybe it's because I love all of the different shades of fall leaves on the trees. Or maybe it's the awesome foods, of course. Whatever it is, it just makes me so happy. If you adore the amazing flavors that come along with this season as much as I do, this section is for you! Fall is such a fun time of year, but as we head into the holiday season, I know it can be harder to stay on track with temptation upon temptation around every corner. These recipes are sure to keep your cravings satisfied and your hunger in check.

Pumpkin Chocolate Chip

This recipe gives you a traditional fall flavor combined with a chocolate surprise in each sip. This is a surefire treat for my fall lovers who also happen to be chocolate lovers. Here's a dash of Halloween to go along with your smoothie!

YIELD: 1 SMOOTHIE

INGREDIENTS

1 serving vanilla protein powder
1 tablespoon (16 g) almond butter
¼ cup (62 g) unsweetened pumpkin puree
1½ teaspoons pumpkin pie spice
¼ teaspoon ground cinnamon
1 cup (192 g) frozen yellow squash
natural sugar substitute to taste
1½ cups (355 ml) unsweetened almond milk
2 teaspoons low-sugar chocolate chips

DIRECTIONS

Place all ingredients except chocolate chips in a blender and blend on high until smooth.

Add chocolate chips and pulse for 15 seconds. Serve.

Sweet Potato Pie

You probably never thought about putting sweet potato in your smoothies, but it's actually an incredible addition. It adds a subtle sweetness and creates a thick, creamy texture that is sure to keep you full for hours. The orange pigment signals that this root vegetable has beta-carotene, which is amazing for our immune system, eyes, and skin!

YIELD: 1 SMOOTHIE

INGREDIENTS

1 serving vanilla protein powder
½ cup (164 g) cooked, cooled sweet potato (no skin)
1 tablespoon (16 g) almond butter
1 tablespoon (13 g) ground flaxseed
1 cup (114 g) cauliflower rice, frozen
1½ teaspoons sugar-free maple syrup
⅛ teaspoon ground cinnamon
1½ cups (355 ml) unsweetened almond milk

DIRECTIONS

Place all ingredients in a blender and blend on high until smooth. Serve.

NOTE If you do not have precooked sweet potatoes, you can microwave a sweet potato for 3 minutes or until fully cooked for a quick option.

Pecan Pie

A staple of Thanksgiving tables for more years than I can count, pecan pie just screams tradition, right? If you're looking to reminisce on some holiday fun, give this a slurp!

YIELD: 1 SMOOTHIE

INGREDIENTS

1 serving vanilla protein powder
¼ cup (28 g) chopped pecans
1½ teaspoons sugar-free maple syrup
1 cup (114 g) cauliflower rice, frozen
1½ cups (355 ml) unsweetened almond milk

DIRECTIONS

Place all ingredients in a blender and blend on high until smooth. Serve.

NOTE Ideally, choose a sugar-free maple syrup that is sweetened with monk fruit, stevia, or erythritol over one sweetened with artificial sugars.

Chai Spice

Starbucks, eat—no, drink—your heart out, because my Chai Spice creation has all the taste of yours, but without the sugar crash! If you're one of my chai latte friends, you'll love this one.

YIELD: 1 SMOOTHIE

INGREDIENTS

1 serving vanilla protein powder
1 tablespoon (16 g) cashew butter
½ teaspoon vanilla extract
½ teaspoon ground cinnamon
¼ teaspoon ground cardamom
¼ teaspoon ground ginger
¼ teaspoon ground clove
¼ teaspoon ground nutmeg
1 cup (114 g) cauliflower rice, frozen
1 cup (237 ml) unsweetened almond milk

DIRECTIONS

Place all ingredients in a blender and blend on high until smooth. Serve.

Apple Cinnamon Crisp

I have always loved the taste of apples, but I used to think they actually made me hungrier. And the truth is that they did, but until I learned about blood sugar balance, I didn't fully understand how that could be prevented. Here's the thing: Alone, an apple will cause a spike and crash in blood sugar, leaving you hungry again soon after. However, when paired with the protein, fat, and fiber like it is in this smoothie, it will keep you full for hours!

YIELD: 1 SMOOTHIE

INGREDIENTS

1 serving vanilla protein powder
1 tablespoon (16 g) almond butter
1 tablespoon (13 g) ground flaxseed
1 apple
½ teaspoon vanilla extract
¼ teaspoon ground cinnamon
1 tablespoon (12 g) sugar-free brown sugar
1 cup (114 g) cauliflower rice, frozen
1½ cups (355 ml) unsweetened almond milk

DIRECTIONS

Place all ingredients in a blender and blend on high until smooth. Serve.

NOTE Ideally, choose a sugar-free brown sugar that is sweetened with monk fruit, stevia, and/or erythritol over one sweetened with artificial sugars.

Almond Pear

This almond pear smoothie is the equivalent of all those unlikely friendships in movies. They seem so bizarre and unconventional, but really, they're perfect together!

YIELD: 1 SMOOTHIE

INGREDIENTS

1 serving vanilla protein powder
1 tablespoon (16 g) almond butter
1 Bartlett pear
1 tablespoon (13 g) ground flaxseed
1 cup (152 g) zucchini, frozen
1½ cups (355 ml) unsweetened vanilla almond milk

DIRECTIONS

Place all ingredients in a blender and blend on high until smooth. Serve.

Carrot Cake

I often get asked whether you can eat carrots while keeping yourself low carb; many people suggest they are very high in sugar. Although carrots may be slightly higher in sugar than other nonstarchy vegetables, it is not something that I would worry about for the average person. Unless you know for a fact that these crunchy orange sticks spike your blood sugar, don't worry about it, doc!

YIELD: 1 SMOOTHIE

INGREDIENTS

1 serving vanilla protein powder
1 tablespoon (16 g) almond butter
6 carrots, or 1½ cups (192 g) chopped carrots (not baby carrots)
½ cup (57 g) cauliflower rice, frozen (if carrots aren't frozen)
1 tablespoon (13 g) ground flaxseed
½ teaspoon vanilla extract
¼ teaspoon ground cinnamon
natural sugar substitute to taste
1¾ cups (420 ml) unsweetened almond milk

DIRECTIONS

Place all ingredients in a blender and blend on high until smooth. Serve.

7

WINTER SMOOTHIES

Winter is coming . . . and so are a bunch of new smoothie recipes! Even though the warm weather might feel far behind us, don't worry. Your smoothie ideas aren't going anywhere! I know that as the weather gets colder, we tend to eat foods that are warmer, and smoothies do thrive best cold. However, with the nutritious and festive high-protein recipes I have created for you in this chapter, we'll be turning up the heat *and* your metabolism to keep you nice and warm.

Chocolate Hazelnut

If you were a fan of paired chocolate and hazelnut while you were growing up, I am confident that this will be a smoothie you'll love. If this winds up being one of your favorites (it's one of mine), I suggest roasting a big batch of hazelnuts in advance. That way, you always have them ready to go for this filling and extremely tasty smoothie.

YIELD: 1 SMOOTHIE

INGREDIENTS

¼ cup (30 g) hazelnuts, roasted and skin removed
1 serving chocolate protein powder
1 tablespoon (5 g) cacao powder
1 cup (152 g) zucchini, frozen
pinch sea salt
natural sugar substitute to taste
1 cup (237 ml) unsweetened almond milk

DIRECTIONS

Preheat oven to 400°F (204°C, gas mark 6). Place hazelnuts on a baking sheet and bake for 10 minutes. Transfer warm hazelnuts to a towel and use the towel to rub the skins off. It doesn't need to be perfect; it's okay if not all the skin is removed.

Place all ingredients in a blender and blend on high until smooth. Serve.

Almond Cookie

This recipe has been an absolute crowd-pleaser among my friends and family for a while now! It tastes like a drinkable version of those Italian almond cookies you might find at your local bakery. This smoothie will help you tackle your cookie cravings in a nutritious and delicious way.

YIELD: 1 SMOOTHIE

INGREDIENTS

1 serving vanilla protein powder
1 tablespoon (16 g) almond butter
1 tablespoon (13 g) ground flaxseed
½ teaspoon almond extract
1 cup (86 g) frozen cauliflower
pinch sea salt
1 cup (237 ml) unsweetened almond milk

DIRECTIONS

Place all ingredients in a blender and blend on high until smooth. Serve.

Sweet Golden Milk

If you're a fan of a turmeric latte, this is the smoothie version for you. Turmeric is the main star of this show, and for a good reason. Its powerful anti-inflammatory properties can help you fight off inflammation and boost your immune system. With colds and flus aplenty going around this time of year, this is the perfect winter treat to keep you healthy all season long.

YIELD: 1 SMOOTHIE

INGREDIENTS

1 serving vanilla protein powder
1 tablespoon (16 g) almond butter
½ frozen banana
1 teaspoon ground turmeric
1 tablespoon (13 g) ground flaxseed
1 cup (192 g) frozen yellow squash
pinch ground black pepper
1½ cups (355 ml) unsweetened almond milk or coconut milk

DIRECTIONS

Place all ingredients in a blender and blend on high until smooth. Serve.

NOTE Pepper helps to activate the curcumin, which is a powerful antioxidant in turmeric.

Sugar Cookie

If you want to taste the equivalent of visiting your grandma's house and smelling a batch of warm cookies right out of the oven, drink this smoothie. This smoothie is cold coziness in edible form!

YIELD: 1 SMOOTHIE

INGREDIENTS

1 serving vanilla protein powder
1 tablespoon (5 g) psyllium husk
1 tablespoon (16 g) cashew butter or (15 ml) melted butter
1 cup (86 g) frozen cauliflower
½ teaspoon vanilla extract
¼ teaspoon butter extract
pinch sea salt
natural sweetener to taste
1½ cups (355 ml) unsweetened almond milk

DIRECTIONS

Place all ingredients in a blender and blend on high until smooth. Serve.

Chocolate Candy Cane

Sleigh all day long with this flavorful, low-carb, high-protein smoothie! If you love a chocolate and peppermint combo, this recipe will help you stay on track with your health goals this holiday season.

YIELD: 1 SMOOTHIE

INGREDIENTS

1 serving chocolate protein powder
1 tablespoon (5 g) cacao powder
1 tablespoon (14 g) cacao butter
1 tablespoon (5 g) psyllium husk
1 cup (114 g) cauliflower rice, frozen
¼ teaspoon peppermint extract
1½ cups (355 ml) unsweetened almond milk

DIRECTIONS

Place all ingredients in a blender and blend on high until smooth. Serve.

NOTE To make the smoothie more like a traditional peppermint, skip the cacao powder and use vanilla protein powder instead!

Popeye's Chocolate-Covered Strawberry

Want to be even stronger than Popeye? Then check out this recipe, which adds protein to his spinach and some chocolate for added fun and flavor! Show yourself—and your muscles—some love with this fruity and chocolate-y protein-packed treat that will have you feeling satiated for hours.

YIELD: 1 SMOOTHIE

INGREDIENTS

1 serving chocolate protein powder
1 tablespoon (5 g) cacao powder
1 tablespoon (16 g) almond butter
1 tablespoon (5 g) psyllium husk
1 cup (140 g) frozen strawberries
½ cup (125 g) frozen spinach
1½ cups (355 ml) unsweetened almond milk

DIRECTIONS

Place all ingredients in a blender and blend on high until smooth. Serve.

Heartthrob Beet Smoothie

What speaks more of love than a gift of health, either to yourself or to someone you care for? And even more than that, you'll . . . beet *. . . surprised at how much of a heartthrob this smoothie becomes for you once you've tasted it!*

YIELD: 1 SMOOTHIE

INGREDIENTS

1 serving vanilla protein powder
½ cup (120 g) cooked and cooled beets, no skin
½ cup (76 g) strawberries or (93 g) blueberries
2 tablespoons (20 g) hemp seeds
1½ cups (355 ml) water

DIRECTIONS

Place all ingredients in a blender and blend on high until smooth. Serve.

Gingerbread

Some people might think adults are too old to make a gingerbread house, but I disagree. Regardless, we're definitely not too old to make gingerbread smoothies! Plus, gingerbread houses are more for show anyway. Sip this delicious gingerbread smoothie for a festive winter treat you can actually taste.

YIELD: 1 SMOOTHIE

INGREDIENTS

1 serving vanilla protein powder
1 tablespoon (16 g) cashew butter
1 tablespoon (13 g) ground flaxseed
½ teaspoon ground cinnamon
½ teaspoon ground ginger
¼ teaspoon allspice
½ teaspoon vanilla extract
1 cup (86 g) frozen cauliflower
pinch sea salt
2 cups (473 ml) unsweetened almond milk

DIRECTIONS

Place all ingredients in a blender and blend on high until smooth. Serve.

8

SMOOTHIE SNACKS

Although a lot of the smoothies I have crafted are designed to be meal replacements, I know that smoothies are also a beloved snack. Don't worry—if having a smoothie snack is the way you want to go, I've got you covered! You can always halve any of the other smoothie recipes in the book to make a snack. However, if your goal is fat loss, I suggest focusing on protein and veggies, keeping fat to a minimum, and skipping the carbs. The smoothies in this book should hold you over for hours, but sometimes you need a snack if you have very large gaps between meals. In this chapter, we will be focusing on protein- and fiber-focused smoothies that will hold you over between meals, if needed.

Cinnamon Swirl

Save yourself a trip to the mall. You'll have all the creamy, cinnamon-y goodness you could ever ask for with this smoothie!

YIELD: 1 SMOOTHIE

INGREDIENTS

1 serving vanilla protein powder
1 cup (114 g) cauliflower rice or (192 g) yellow squash, frozen
½ teaspoon vanilla extract
1 teaspoon ground cinnamon
1 cup (237 ml) unsweetened almond milk
natural sugar substitute to taste

DIRECTIONS

Place all ingredients in a blender and blend on high until smooth.

Optional: Dust with cinnamon. Serve.

Hot Chocolate

Served hot or cold, this smoothie will satisfy your chocolate craving all year round! This is my go-to snack if I want something sweet but need a little protein boost to shut down my hunger.

YIELD: 1 SMOOTHIE

INGREDIENTS

½ serving chocolate protein powder
2 teaspoons cacao powder
½ teaspoon vanilla extract
¼ teaspoon ground cinnamon
pinch sea salt
natural sugar substitute to taste
1 cup (237 ml) unsweetened vanilla almond milk

DIRECTIONS

Place all ingredients in a blender and blend on high until smooth.

Enjoy smoothie cold or heat it over the stove for a warm beverage!

Coffee Date

Unlike some dates you may have been on in the past, this smoothie is sure to not disappoint. This slightly sweet beverage is the perfect snack to get you through the day.

YIELD: 1 SMOOTHIE

INGREDIENTS

1 serving vanilla protein powder
1 cup (237 ml) cold-brew coffee
½ cup (118 ml) unsweetened almond milk
1 small date
¼ teaspoon ground cinnamon
½ teaspoon vanilla extract
½ cup (118 ml) ice

DIRECTIONS

Place all ingredients in a blender and blend on high until smooth. Serve.

Matcha Green Tea

In the mood for a matcha latte? I've gotta give my sister credit for this creation—a much more blood sugar–friendly version of a matcha latte that I just had to share with you. This high-protein snack is packed with antioxidants and L-theanine, which will give you a steadier energy than coffee will and keep you focused and full for hours. Skip the crash from the sugar and the caffeine with this smoothie!

YIELD: 1 SMOOTHIE

INGREDIENTS

1 serving vanilla protein powder
1 tablespoon (6 g) matcha powder
natural sugar substitute to taste
1 cup (237 ml) unsweetened coconut milk

DIRECTIONS

Place all ingredients in a blender and blend on high until smooth. Serve.

Lemon Ginger

The smoothie is refreshing and tartlike, with an energizing, tangy zest! It has a kick to it that is perfect for when you want a snack to light you up.

YIELD: 1 SMOOTHIE

INGREDIENTS

1 serving vanilla protein powder
juice of 1 lemon
zest of ¼ lemon
1-inch (2.5 cm) piece ginger or 1 teaspoon minced ginger
1 cup (114 g) cauliflower rice, frozen
1 cup (237 ml) cold water

DIRECTIONS

Place all ingredients in a blender and blend on high until smooth. Serve.